States

LOUISIANA

by Angie Swanson

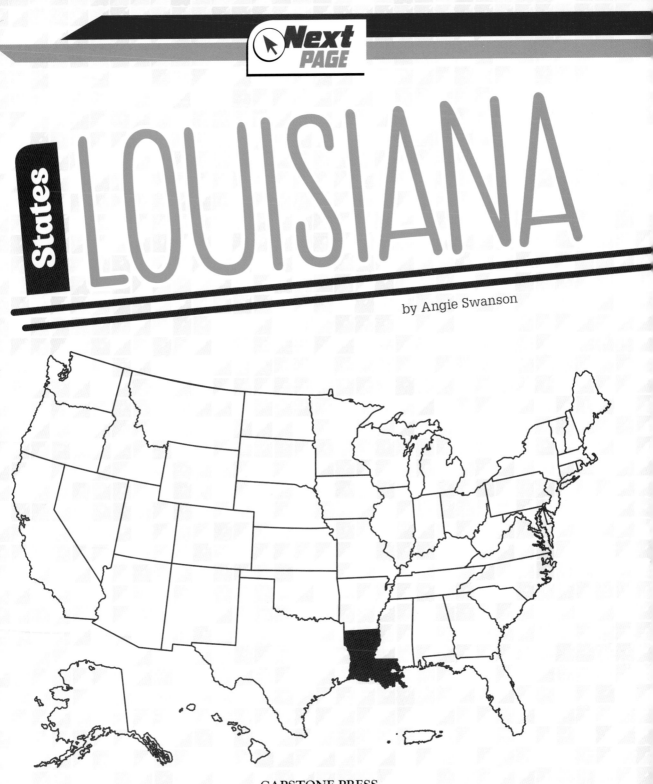

CAPSTONE PRESS
a capstone imprint

Next Page Books are published by Capstone Press,
1710 Roe Crest Drive, North Mankato, Minnesota 56003
www.mycapstone.com

Library of Congress Cataloging-in-Publication Data
Cataloging-in-publication information is on file with the Library of
Congress.
ISBN 978-1-5157-0405-8 (library binding)
ISBN 978-1-5157-0464-5 (paperback)
ISBN 978-1-5157-0516-1 (ebook PDF)

Editorial Credits
Jaclyn Jaycox, editor; Kazuko Collins and Katy LaVigne, designers;
Morgan Walters, media researcher; Laura Manthe, production specialist

Photo Credits
Capstone Press: Angi Gahler, map 4, 7; CriaImages.com: Jay Robert
Nash Collection, top 18; Getty Images: DEA / G. DAGLI ORTI, 12, 25,
Ed Vebell, 26, sacherjj, 28; iStockphoto: Coast-to-Coast, bottom left
21; Newscom: Jeff Malet Photography, bottom 18; One Mile Up, Inc.,
flag, seal 23; Shutterstock: Action Sports Photography, bottom 24,
Aleksey Stemmer, bottom right 21, Aneese, 10, Bos11, top left 20,
Chuck Wagner, 14, 29, Colin D. Young, bottom right 8, Daniel Prudek,
bottom right 20, Don Mammoser, middle right 21, Everett Historical,
27, f11photo, 5, Fotoluminate LLC, 9, Gordon Logue, top 24, Helga
Esteb, top 19, Hysteria, top left 21, Joe Seer, middle 18, Joseph Sohm,
17, Kenneth Keifer, bottom left 20, Nagel Photography, 13, Pierre-
Jean Durieu, 6, 16, Randy Miramontez, bottom 19, RIRF Stock, 11,
robcocquyt, 15, s_bukley, middle 19, Stephen Helstowski, bottom left
8, Steve Bower, 7, Tom Reichner, top right 21, torm, middle left 21,
Virunja, top right 20, Warren Price Photography, cover

All design elements by Shutterstock

Printed and bound in China.
0316/CA21600187
012016   009436F16

TABLE OF CONTENTS

Want to take your research further? Ask your librarian if your school subscribes to PebbleGo Next. If so, when you see this helpful symbol 🔎 throughout the book, log onto www.pebblegonext.com for bonus downloads and information.

LOCATION

Louisiana is a southern state. Texas borders it on the west. Arkansas lies to the north. The Mississippi River forms the border between Louisiana and the state of Mississippi on the east. The Gulf of Mexico lies to the south. Louisiana's capital, Baton Rouge, is on the Mississippi River. The state's largest cities are New Orleans, Baton Rouge, and Shreveport.

PebbleGo Next Bonus! To print and label your own map, go to www.pebblegonext.com and search keywords:

LA MAP

The Mississippi River gives New Orleans a moon-like shape. It's nicknamed "The Crescent City."

GEOGRAPHY

The Mississippi River brings silt to Louisiana. Sand, dirt, and other materials the river carries are called alluvial deposits. These deposits increase the land size. Most of Louisiana was created thousands of years ago by the Mississippi River deposits.

Eastern Louisiana is filled with marshes that lie barely above sea level. Marshlands also cover the rest of the coastal region.

The northwestern part of the state has several forests and state parks. In this region is Louisiana's only mountain and highest point. Driskill Mountain is 535 feet (163 meters) above sea level.

PebbleGo Next Bonus! To watch a video about crawfishing, go to www.pebblegonext.com and search keywords:
LA VIDEO

A steamboat leaves the Port of New Orleans, located on the Mississippi River.

Swamps and lowlands are found along the coast and eastern part of Louisiana.

Legend

▲ Highest Point

Lake

National Park

River

Kisatchie National Forest

▲ Driskill Mountain

Kisatchie National Forest—

Kisatchie National Forest

Red River

Lake Bruin

Catahoula Lake

Mississippi River

Pearl River

N W E S

Atchafalaya River

WEST GULF COASTAL PLAIN

MISSISSIPPI RIVER ALLUVIAL PLAIN

EAST GULF COASTAL PLAIN

Lake Pontchartrain

Chandeleur Sound

Sabine River

Sabine Lake

GULF COAST REGION

Calcasieu Lake

New Orleans Jazz National Park

Breton Sound

Atchafalaya Bay

Scale
Miles
0   25   50   75   100
0 25 50 75 100
Kilometers

Gulf of Mexico

WEATHER

The Gulf of Mexico brings warm air and moisture to Louisiana. This air keeps Louisiana hot in the summer and warm the rest of the year. The state's average summer temperature is 81 degrees Fahrenheit (27 degrees Celsius). Its average winter temperature is 51°F (11°C).

Average High and Low Temperatures (New Orleans, LA)

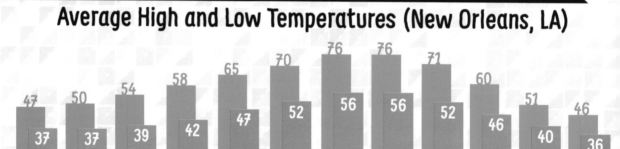

	JAN	FEB	MAR	APR	MAY	JUN	JUL	AUG	SEP	OCT	NOV	DEC
High	47	50	54	58	65	70	76	76	71	60	51	46
Low	37	37	39	42	47	52	56	56	52	46	40	36

LANDMARKS

Jackson Square

Jackson Square is in the middle of New Orleans' oldest neighborhood, the French Quarter. Artists often display their work outside in the Square. A statue of Andrew Jackson on a horse is featured in front of St. Louis Cathedral, a church that was built in 1727. The statue honors Jackson's victory in the Battle of New Orleans. Jackson Square was declared a National Historic Landmark in 1960.

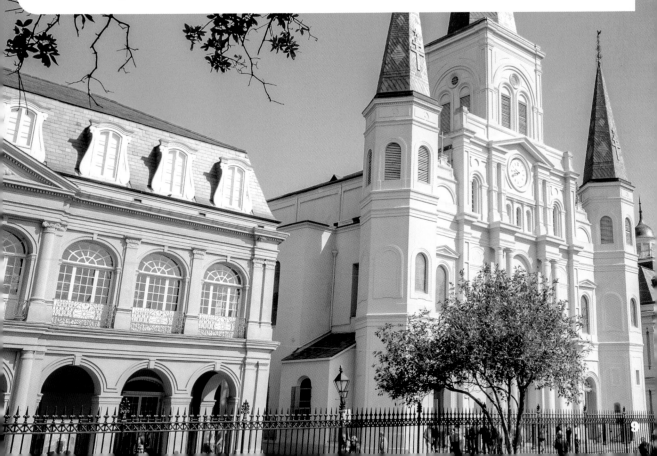

Superdome

The Superdome in New Orleans opened in 1975. The New Orleans Saints of the NFL play their home games in this dome. The Super Bowl has been played there seven times. Major college bowl games, concerts, and other large events have also been held there. The Superdome was damaged in Hurricane Katrina and reopened a year later.

Lake Pontchartrain

Lake Pontchartrain is Louisiana's largest lake. It lies east of the Mississippi River and borders New Orleans. The lake is a popular fishing destination. The 23.83-mile (38.35-kilometer) causeway that crosses the lake is the world's longest bridge over water.

INDUSTRY

Louisiana is one of the largest oil-producing states. Louisiana also produces natural gas and gasohol fuel, which is safer for the environment than gasoline. Petrochemical products are another important industry. These products are made from petroleum or natural gas. Of these, rubber is the most common.

Other natural resources help Louisiana's industry. Sugarcane is Louisiana's largest agricultural product. Louisiana's hot weather is good for growing sweet potatoes, rice, cotton, and pecans. Shrimp is Louisiana's most profitable seafood industry. Fishers trap crawfish in rivers, swamps, and bayous. Farmers also raise crawfish in ponds.

One out of every 70 jobs in Louisiana is related to the seafood industry.

Tourism is a large part of Louisiana's economy. Tourists go to New Orleans for Mardi Gras. This celebration is held 47 days before Easter Sunday. Travelers enjoy seeing the French Quarter in New Orleans. Performers juggle, dance, and play music for visitors walking along streets.

An oil rig pumps oil off the coast of Louisiana.

POPULATION

Louisiana is a land of many cultures. French, British, Spanish, Haitian, and African ancestors created a special culture in Louisiana. Many residents have Italian, German, Irish, or other European roots. Almost one-third of Louisianans are African-American. Hispanics make up about 4 percent of the population. Most of Louisiana's American Indians live near the southeast coast.

Many Louisianans call themselves Creole or Cajun. Creole usually refers to anyone in Louisiana with French or Spanish ancestors. Some people only use the term to refer to those whose ancestors came to Louisiana directly from France. Cajuns are the descendants of the French people who moved to Louisiana from Canada or the northern states.

Population by Ethnicity

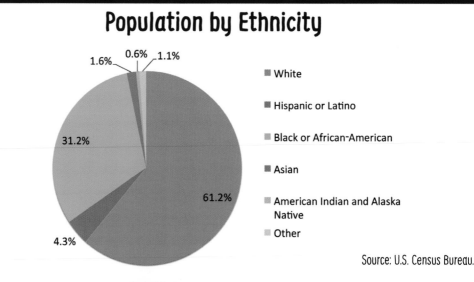

1.6% 0.6% 1.1%

31.2%

4.3%

61.2%

- White
- Hispanic or Latino
- Black or African-American
- Asian
- American Indian and Alaska Native
- Other

Source: U.S. Census Bureau.

The annual Mardi Gras celebration in New Orleans typically draws more than 1 million people.

FAMOUS PEOPLE

Louis Armstrong (1901–1971) was a famous jazz trumpet player and singer. He was born in New Orleans.

Harry Connick Jr. (1967–) is a singer, pianist, and actor. He was born in New Orleans.

William Joyce (1957–) has written and illustrated dozens of children's books. He has also created animated TV shows and movies. He was one of the producers of the 2005 movie *Robots*. His book *The Leaf Men and the Brave Good Bugs* was adapted into a 2013 computer-animated movie, *Epic*. He was born in Shreveport.

Ellen Degeneres (1958–) is a comedian and actor. She has hosted an award-winning talk show, *The Ellen DeGeneres Show*, since 2003. She was born in Metairie.

Peyton Manning (1976–) is an NFL quarterback and five-time league Most Valuable Player. Born in New Orleans, he played 13 years for the Indianapolis Colts, where he helped the team win Super Bowl XLI. In 2015 with the Denver Broncos, he passed Brett Favre for having the most career passing yards in NFL history.

Lil Wayne (1982–) is a Grammy award–winning rapper. He was born Dwayne Michael Carter Jr. in New Orleans.

STATE SYMBOLS

Tree

bald cypress

Flower

magnolia

Bird

eastern brown pelican

Insect

honeybee

PebbleGo Next Bonus! To make a dessert using praline pecans, go to www.pebblegonext.com and search keywords:

LA RECIPE

Dog

Catahoula leopard dog

Animal

black bear

Reptile

alligator

Amphibian

green tree frog

Fish

white perch

Crustacean

crawfish

MINING PRODUCTS
natural gas, petroleum, coal, salt

MANUFACTURED GOODS
petroleum and coal products, chemicals, food and beverage products

FARM PRODUCTS
rice, sugar, corn, cotton, potatoes, tobacco, crawfish

PROFESSIONAL SPORTS TEAMS
New Orleans Pelicans (NBA)
New Orleans Saints (NFL)

PebbleGo Next Bonus!
To learn the lyrics to
the state song, go to
www.pebblegonext.com
and search keywords:

LA SONG

LOUISIANA TIMELINE

1519 — Alonso Alvarez de Pineda explores the Gulf Coast from Florida to Texas and claims the entire area for Spain.

1682 — René-Robert Cavalier, known as Sieur de la Salle, claims the Louisiana area for France and calls it Louisiana in honor of King Louis XIV.

1715 — Louis Juchereau de Saint-Denis establishes the first permanent settlement in Louisiana.

1718 — New Orleans is founded.

1762 — King Louis XV of France gives New Orleans and the land west of it to his cousin, King Charles III of Spain.

1763 France turned over the area east of New Orleans to England after the Seven Years' War (1756–1763) between England and France.

1764 French Canadians known as Acadians arrive in Louisiana. Today these people are known as Cajuns.

1775–1783 The American colonies fight for independence from Great Britain in the Revolutionary War.

1779 Spanish soldiers and American volunteers help keep Baton Rouge from being captured by the British during the Revolutionary War.

1803 U.S. President Thomas Jefferson purchases Louisiana Territory from France.

 **1812** On April 30 Louisiana becomes the 18th state.

 1815 In January General Andrew Jackson beats the British in the Battle of New Orleans. This was the last battle of the War of 1812 (1812–1815).

1849 The capital city moves from New Orleans to Baton Rouge after a statewide vote.

1861–1865 The Union and the Confederacy fight the Civil War; Louisiana fights for the Confederacy.

 **1862** Louisiana is occupied by Union troops.

 **1865** Convention of Colored Men is formed. This group encouraged Louisiana to adopt a Black Code that gave African-American men rights such as owning property.

1901 The state's first oil field is discovered near Jennings.

1914–1918 World War I is fought; the United States enters the war in 1917.

1916 Natural gas is discovered near Monroe.

1960 New Orleans begins to desegregate its public schools. Before this time African-Americans and whites had attended separate schools.

1975 The Superdome sports stadium opens in New Orleans.

1977 Ernest Morial is elected the first black mayor of New Orleans.

1984 The World's Fair is held in New Orleans.

2005 On August 29 Hurricane Katrina strikes southeastern Louisiana, damaging levees and flooding New Orleans; about 2,000 people are killed in the disaster.

2010 On April 20, 11 people are killed and 17 injured when a British Petroleum (BP) offshore oil rig in the Gulf of Mexico explodes; 210 million gallons (795 million liters) of oil spill into the Gulf. By June oil washes ashore on Louisiana's coast, damaging the wildlife.

2013 On February 3 the Super Bowl is played in the Superdome in New Orleans; hosting this big game shows the country that the city is recovering from Hurricane Katrina.

2015 Hurricane Patricia becomes the strongest Pacific hurricane on record; it causes dangerous flooding in Louisiana.

Glossary

bayou *(BYE-oo)*—a stream that runs slowly through a swamp and leads to or from a lake or river

culture *(KUHL-chur)*—the way of life, ideas, customs, and traditions of a group of people

executive *(ig-ZE-kyuh-tiv)*—the branch of government that makes sure laws are followed

industry *(IN-duh-stree)*—a business which produces a product or provides a service

legislature *(LEJ-iss-lay-chur)*—a group of elected officials who have the power to make or change laws for a country or state

marsh *(MARSH)*—an area of wet, low land usually covered in grasses and low plants

petroleum *(puh-TROH-lee-uhm)*—an oily liquid found below the earth's surface used to make gasoline, heating oil, and many other products

region *(REE-juhn)*—a large area

sea level *(SEE LEV-uhl)*—the average level of the surface of the ocean, used as a starting point from which to measure the height or depth of any place

silt *(SILT)*—the fine particles of soil that are carried along by flowing water and eventually settle to the bottom of a river or lake

Read More

Bjorklund, Ruth. *Louisiana.* It's My State! New York: Cavendish Square Publishing, 2014.

Felix, Rebecca. *What's Great About Louisiana?* Our Great States. Minneapolis: Lerner Publications, 2016.

Ganeri, Anita. *United States of America: A Benjamin Blog and His Inquisitive Dog Guide.* Country Guides. Chicago: Heinemann Raintree, 2015.

Internet Sites

FactHound offers a safe, fun way to find Internet sites related to this book. All of the sites on FactHound have been researched by our staff.

Here's all you do:

Visit *www.facthound.com*

Type in this code: 9781515704058

Super-cool stuff! Check out projects, games and lots more at
www.capstonekids.com

Critical Thinking Using the Common Core

1. What is the difference between Creole and Cajun? (Key Ideas and Details)

2. Mardi Gras is a huge celebration in New Orleans. Why is this event important for Louisiana's economy? (Integration of Knowledge and Ideas)

3. Due to the amount of swamps and marshes in Louisiana, bayous are common. What is a bayou? Hint: Use the glossary for help. (Craft and Structure)

Index